MICROGREENS BUSINESS

A COMPLETE STEP BY STEP GUIDE FOR GROWING MICROGREENS INDOOR AND RUNNING A PROFITABLE BUSINESS WITH LIMITED SPACE, TIME AND MONEY

RONALD LEE MASON

MICROGREENS BUSINESS

Copyright © 2021 RONALD LEE MASON

All rights reserved

Independently published

ISBN: 9798530057656

This book is for someone who believed in me.

MICROGREENS BUSINESS

LEGAL NOTICE:

All rights reserved. No part of this book may be reproduced or transmitted in any form or by any means, electronic or mechanical, including photocopying, recording, or by an information storage and retrieval system - except by a reviewer who may quote brief passages in a review to be printed in a magazine - or newspaper - without permission in writing from the publisher.

The Publisher has strived to be as accurate and complete as possible in the creation of this book, notwithstanding the fact that he does not warrant or represent at any time that the contents within are accurate due to the rapidly changing nature of the Internet.

While all attempts have been made to verify information provided in this publication, the Publisher assumes no responsibility for errors, omissions, or contrary interpretation of the subject matter herein. Any perceived slights of specific persons, peoples, or organizations are unintentional.

In practical advice books, like anything else in life, there are no guarantees of income made. Readers are cautioned to reply on their own judgment about their individual circumstances to act accordingly.

This book is not intended for use as a source of legal, business, accounting or financial advice. All readers are advised to seek services of competent professionals in legal, business, accounting, and finance field.

TABLE OF CONTENTS

PREFACE 11
INTRODUCTION TO MICROGREENS 15
    What are microgreens 15
    Nutritional values of microgreens 17
    Microgreens' health benefits 18
WHY START A MICROGREENS BUSINESS 23
    The market grows 23
    Low investment cost 24
    It is a local business 25
    Short productive periods 26
    All-year-round production 26
    High monetary value 27
COMMON QUESTIONS ABOUT MICROGREENS BUSINESS . 29
    How much space do you need? 29
    How much you can earn? 30
    How long does this business take? 30
    Do You need a license to sell microgreens? 31
    Is this business right for you? 32

MICROGREENS BUSINESS

FINDING YOUR NICHE 34
The best microgreens to grow 35
GROWING MICROGREENS 38
Soil Method: step by step instructions 40
Step 1: soaking 41
Step 2: preparing the grow tray 42
Step 3: planting 43
Step 4: covering 44
Step 5: maintenance 45
Step 6: uncovering 46
Step 7: growing 47
Step 8: harvesting 48
Step 9: Storing 49
Hydroponic method 50
Will microgreens regrow? 52
COMMON PROBLEMS (AND HOW TO SOLVE THEM) 53
Clumpy microgreens 54
Uneven growth 54
Mold 55
Fungus 56
Slow germination 57
Bad quality water 58
Overwatering 60

- Poor ventilation 60
- Plants keep falling over 61

HYGIENE AND FOOD SAFETY REGULATIONS 63
- Identify the laws in your area 64
- Food Safety Modernization Act 64
- Good Agricultural Practices 65

HOW TO SET UP A SMALL VERTICAL FARM 69
- Shelving system 71
- Led Grow Lights 72
- USB fans 74
- Microgreen trays 76
- Cost estimates 77
- Profit estimates 78

MARKETING MICROGREENS 83
- My microgreens are so good, but no one knows it 85
- The importance of marketing planning 87

DISTRIBUTION 89
- Where to sell microgreens 90
  - Restaurants 90
  - Grocery stores 92
  - Farmer's markets 93
  - Direct sales 94

BRANDING 97

MICROGREENS BUSINESS

    Logo 98

    Marketing Informational Materials 99

PRICING 101

PACKAGING 105

    Labelling 110

    Barcodes 114

MAKE YOUR DREAM HAPPEN! 117

APPENDIX: MOST POPULAR MICROGREENS 121

    1. Sunflower 123

    2. Pea 124

    3. Broccoli 125

    4. Basil 126

    5. Cress 127

    6. Radish 128

    7. Arugula 129

    8. Cilantro/Coriander 130

    9. Amaranth 131

    10. Beet 132

    11. Borage 133

    12. Cabbage (Cauliflower) 134

    13. Kohlrabi 135

    14. Turnip 136

    15. Onion 137

MICROGREENS BUSINESS

16. Fennel 138
17. Mustard – Spinach (Komatsuna) 139
18. Mizuna 140
19. Nasturtium 141
20. Tatsoi 142

PREFACE

Have you ever thought about starting a new business that doesn't require a lot of time, space, and investment? In this book, I want to tell you about this new business idea that can allow you to make a thousand dollars or more a week.

Microgreens are a new category of vegetables that are harvested shortly after the first set of true leaves form. Some chefs in California have been using them since the mid-1980s, but the demand for microgreens has only recently grown exponentially. That's because microgreens are healthy foods that contain many more nutrients than plants harvested at an advanced stage of maturity. For this reason, they are recommended by nutritionists and are popular among healthy lifestyle followers and environmentally conscious people.

MICROGREENS BUSINESS

Many think they can't become microgreens farmers because they either don't have a green thumb or aren't good at business.

As for the first point, I can tell you that I did it - I didn't even have a houseplant before - and I'm sure you will too. Growing microgreens is quick and easy, with most microgreen varieties reaching a harvestable size in about two weeks, so you can grow up to two dozen plants in a year.

Only some basic equipment is needed, and you don't have to worry too much about the plants. You can grow microgreens in a spare room of your house or in a small garage. The activities required for this are limited to sowing the seeds and a few waterings.

Once or twice a week, you can harvest and sell your microgreens (later in the book, I explain who you can sell them to and how to do that).

As for your business skills, it's true: you need to have some inclination to sell, but you can learn that quickly. I've done a lot of trial and error, but I hadn't read a book like this. You will avoid the mistakes I made, and my advice will give you a significant advantage. In any case, I must point out that this is a business you should run on a small scale. So once you have the few customers necessary to run your business, you can move on without too much difficulty.

At first, the idea of starting this business can be intimidating, but you'll have to take my word for it: there is a booming market that is constantly (and increasingly) demanding these products. Once word gets out, you'll be amazed at how many people will ask you to buy the product. In this book, I tell you which microgreens are best to start with, which are the easiest to grow, and which are the most difficult. If you follow my advice, success won't be too hard.

Microgreens can be grown in soil or hydroponically. In this book, you will find step-by-step instructions for both growing methods. I'll also show you how to build a grow rack with readily available components without breaking the bank. In addition, I will provide you with blueprints to set up a proper vertical farm in a small 60 square foot space.

Finally, I'll explain how to do everything involved with your business from identifying your market niche to identifying your customers to product packaging, pricing and marketing.

If you have no intention of selling your products but are curious to learn more about microgreens, I definitely recommend reading the book because this is not just a business book. Like I said, microgreens are incredible foods that are great for your health and are not easy to find on the market. By reading this volume, you will learn how to grow them yourself at home. This way, you will always have a very fresh product with unique properties available for your consumption.

MICROGREENS BUSINESS

What are you waiting for to get started? Start reading the book now. The world of microgreens will soon have no more secrets for you!

INTRODUCTION TO MICROGREENS

What are microgreens

Microgreens are young and tender seedlings of various vegetables, wild plants and herbs. They are optimal when harvested only 7-20 days after sowing, at which time they develop the first true leaves, namely the two cotyledons.

We cannot define them as sprouts, as is wholly and often wrong, and they are not even ordinary leafy vegetables. They are a new category of vegetables that guarantee an early harvest and are perfect for building a limited growing system.

They are loved and used by more and more chefs and cooks because they are flavorful and add unexpected beauty and texture to dishes. They are increasingly in demand by consumers because they are good to eat, enjoyable to look at and very nutritious.

They are rich in minerals, vitamins and have antioxidant compounds that are vital for human health. The researchers of the University of Maryland[1] found that micro-vegetables have a high content of bioactive substances (10 times higher than ordinary vegetables) and improve digestive activity and defend our body. That is why they are called superfoods, and especially why I want to show you how to grow them at home. Microgreens are sometimes available in specialised supermarkets, but it is always better to grow them yourself and with little effort. If you read this book, you will understand that microgreens can also be a great business that does not require a significant investment, much space or even time.

As mentioned earlier, one aspect that makes microgreens unique and distinctive from both a gastronomic and nutritional perspective is the variety of produce, shapes, flavours, and colours you can find.

Note: Microgreens have nothing to do with GMOs (Genetically Modified Organisms). Microgreens result from

---

[1] Lester, Gene & Xiao, Zhenlei & Luo, Yaguang & Wang, Qin. (2013). Microgreens: Assessment of Nutrient Concentrations.

research on traditional cabbage, squash, green beans, spinach, broccoli, and more.

Therefore, we can expect that these products will increasingly form the basis of our diet in the future, as they are easy to grow even in an urban environment, using the system of vertical farms or indoor cultivation in grow boxes with the help of LED lights.

Nutritional values of microgreens

Microgreens are one of the superfoods or functional foods. These vegetables are high in minerals (Ca, Mg, Fe, Mn, Zn, Se, Mo), vitamins (α-tocopherol/vitamin E, β-carotene/pro-vitamin A, ascorbic acid/vitamin C and phylloquinone/vitamin K1) and bioactive compounds such as phenolic antioxidants, anthocyanins, glucosinolates and carotenoids.

Recent studies[2] have shown that the bioactive compounds in micro vegetables were richer in phenolic antioxidants and more significant amounts of α-tocopherol and carotenoids than the adult versions of the plants. Broccoli

---

[2] Zhenlei Xiao, Gene E. Lester, Yaguang Luo, and Qin Wang, "Assessment of Vitamin and Carotenoid Concentrations of Emerging Food Products: Edible Microgreens", *Journal of Agricultural and Food Chemistry*, July 18, 2012.

and lettuce had the highest amounts of vitamin E, while Asteraceae showed the highest carotenoid levels.

As a pure example, the vitamin C in a microgreen can be six times higher than that contained in the same adult plant. The amount of vitamin K can be 60 times more significant, and vitamin E can be as much as 400 times greater. From this, it is easy to deduce that taking much smaller amounts of the product is sufficient to get the recommended daily doses of these three vitamins.

To complete the example, an adult of average weight would need only 0,5 oz of red cabbage for the recommended daily requirement of vitamin E, only 1,4 oz of red cabbage for the recommended daily requirement of vitamin C, and only 0,6 oz of amaranth for the recommended daily requirement of vitamin K.

Microgreens' health benefits

Many of us were told as children to "eat our greens." By and large, there is a scientific consensus that a balanced, rotating diet of different vegetables is one of the best ways to get nutrients from food at a young age.

Being low in calories but high in nutrients, most health experts recommend eating vegetables daily.

So, if it is known that vegetables are good for you, it is even more true for microgreens.

Just as there are studies that show microgreens have high nutritional value, others provide evidence that the high levels of nutrients in microgreens can lead to significant health benefits.

Here are just a few examples of the benefits microgreens can bring to the health of those who eat them.

Microgreens lower the risk of cardiovascular disease.

This is because they can lower levels of low-density lipoprotein (LDL) cholesterol. This is often referred to as "bad" cholesterol because too high a level can increase the risk of heart attack, stroke, and other cardiovascular diseases.

Microgreens lower thre risk of Alzheimer's disease.

Oxidative stress in the body can cause or exacerbate many diseases, Alzheimer's being a prime example. Microgreens contain antioxidant-rich components like sulforaphane, which reduces the risk of Alzheimer's disease. Researchers have found that a pure sulforaphane extract can protect against oxidative stress and inflammation of the brain. Researchers also found that sulforaphane may protect against memory deficits symptomatic of Alzheimer's disease[3].

Microgreens help with diabetic control.

Microgreens (like other vegetables) are particularly rich in fibre, which is needed for optimal digestion. They have a low glycemic index, so your blood sugar doesn't rise quickly after a meal. The American Diabetes Association recommends at least 3 to 5 servings of non-starchy vegetables like broccoli, carrots or cauliflower per day.

Microgreens can reduce cancer risk.

Some studies[4] have shown that the bioactive antioxidant compounds present in many microgreens reduce tumour cell proliferation by up to 41.9%. Therefore, daily

---

[3] Lee S, Choi BR, Kim J, LaFerla FM, Park JHY, Han JS, Lee KW, Kim J. Sulforaphane Upregulates the Heat Shock Protein Co-Chaperone CHIP and Clears Amyloid-β and Tau in a Mouse Model of Alzheimer's Disease. Mol Nutr Food Res. 2018 Jun;62(12):e1800240. doi: 10.1002/mnfr.201800240. Epub 2018 May 28. PMID: 29714053.

[4] Beatriz de la Fuente, Gabriel López-García, Vicent Máñez, Amparo Alegría, Reyes Barberá, and Antonio Cilla, "Antiproliferative Effect of Bioaccessible Fractions of Four Brassicaceae Microgreens on Human Colon Cancer Cells Linked to Their Phytochemical Composition", *Antioxidants* (Basel). 2020 May; 9(5): 368.

consumption of microgreens as part of a balanced diet could be a preventative nutritional strategy to reduce the burden of chronic degenerative diseases such as colon cancer.

The health benefits listed above are widely supported by the latest scientific research and can explain the success of these products.

The fact is that microgreens are not only beautiful and good, they are also good for your health.

MICROGREENS BUSINESS

WHY START A MICROGREENS BUSINESS

There are many good reasons to start a microgreen business:

The market grows

The pandemic COVID-19 has changed people's consumption habits. Microgreens have no direct impact on the virus but are good for health due to their nutritional properties. Consumers in the Western world are increasingly asking for this type of produce.

In many countries, microgreens are well known and used, especially in gourmet cuisine. These tiny plants can be an innovative and unique ingredient capable of enhancing dishes beyond aesthetics by adding flavour (microgreens enrich dishes with distinctive flavours, from sweet to salty, to spicy and sharp-tasting) and, most importantly, by increasing the nutritional value of food.

Microgreens are also increasingly used in cosmetics to make shampoos and skincare products. Consequently, the industrial demand for these products is also growing.

Recent research forecasts a steady growth of 7.5% per annum for the microgreens market. This growth trend is expected to continue at least until 2026[5].

The key sales markets are the United States, followed by Canada and Mexico, but demand for microgreens is also significant in Europe.

Low investment cost

You can start your business with a few trays, some soil and a few seeds and go from there. All the materials needed to

---

[5] Microgreens Market - Growth, Trends, COVID-19 Impact, and Forecasts (2021 - 2026), Mordor Intelligence, April 2021, ID: 4987100.

grow a single plant can cost about two dollars.

With a few hundred dollars, you can buy all the materials you need to build a grow rack (as I will show you later in the book) and start growing microgreens on a larger scale. Most of the materials like racks, soil, and trays are also reusable. The other materials used in microgreens production, such as seeds and packaging, are not overly expensive, especially compared to the price to sell the produce. It is possible to recoup the investment costs in a short time fully.

It is a local business

Since this is a relatively new business, there are no significant manufacturers in the market yet. Also, the product is inherently suited to be marketed by local farmers who can make better contact with restaurants and small shops in the area.

As you test your technique and specialize, you can make free samples and distribute them at restaurants, bars, grocery stores, and farmers markets. You don't have to struggle to become a top distributor. You can gradually grow your business and increase your production as demand grows.

Short productive periods

Unlike most adult plants, the production cycle of microgreens is manageable. It takes between one and four weeks from sowing to harvest, depending on the variety.

Such a short production cycle allows the inexperienced grower to learn and specialize in a short time, identify and reduce common problems, and maximize production and efficiency. You can quickly increase or decrease output as your sales fluctuate throughout the year.

All-year-round production

Unlike most crops, microgreens can be grown even during winter in northern climate zones.

This is undoubtedly a great advantage for anyone who wants to start a business. Many microgreens' farmers I know to work in regions of the world where nothing else can be grown or can only be grown for a few months a year. Microgreens don't see this problem. All you need is a room that is not too cold and LED lights that simulate solar lighting. With these simple means, you can grow all year round without problems.

MICROGREENS BUSINESS

High monetary value.

Microgreens are niche products targeted to an audience of people who care about the environment and their health.

Consumers worldwide are voting with their wallets for local food, choosing to seek out and buy from local growers instead of buying food that is transported hundreds or even thousands of miles. This need creates new opportunities for small farmers to start or expand their businesses.

There is still not enough supply in the market to meet demand.

Due to the high nutritional content of many microgreens, holistic doctors and nutritionists are now beginning to recommend microgreens to their patients. In addition, microgreens are also starting to become very popular in the cosmetic industry.

Because microgreens bring such a high price, typically $20 to $30 per pound, growers can get a quick return on their investment for equipment, seed and labor.

These elements make it possible to apply a premium price and make microgreens a product with a high retail value.

MICROGREENS BUSINESS

When you combine consistent sales strategies and increasingly efficient production, you can break even in a short period and make a large profit margin.

COMMON QUESTIONS ABOUT MICROGREENS BUSINESS

How much space do you need?

Growing microgreens doesn't require much space. If you have a spare room in your house, that's more than enough space to get started. Most microgreens growers use racks to make the most of vertical space.

MICROGREENS BUSINESS

How much you can earn?

The average selling price for microgreens is $25 – 40 per pound. If you are starting and growing microgreens on a single level, such as a table, each 10" x 20" tray will generally produce 8 to 12 ounces of microgreens, depending on what you are growing. That means you will be able to earn at least $12.5 – 18.8 per tray of microgreens.

Many growers can produce 50 pounds of microgreens per 2-week cycle in a 60-square-foot room using racks with four compartments. At $25 per pound, that's $1,250 per cycle, or about $2,500 per month. At $40 per pound, that's $2.000 per cycle or about $4.000 per month.

So once your operation is up and running, you can make $41 - $66 per square foot each month.

How long does this business take?

The amount of time you need to spend per week on your microgreen business depends on the size of your business.

If you're only growing a dozen floors a week in a side room, then it may be a part-time job that only takes 15 to 30 minutes every other day, plus a little extra time for harvesting and selling.

If you're running a six-figure (or more!) microgreens operation, expect it to be a full-time job plus something else.

You'll probably need to hire a few employees to keep up with demand.

So basically, a microgreens business can take as much or as little time as you want. As in most areas of life, you will get a proportional amount compared to what you put into it.

There are some economies of scale that you can use to your advantage.

Do You need a license to sell microgreens?

One of the most common questions people ask about this business is whether they need to get some license or certification or go through the government to sell microgreens. The answer is that it depends on where you are located.

We'll cover this topic in more detail in a later chapter of the book. In the meantime, however, I can tell you that every state in America has its own rules, and to find out what the rules are in your state (if you live in the U.S.), you can visit your state's Department of Agriculture websites. For example, when I started my business, the first thing I did was register with the state as a business and get my brand name for a people farm, and that made me a legal business. Then I did much research in my state's Department of Agriculture and found almost nothing about microgreens. I talked to some lawyers, and they told me that in my state, you are exempt from nearly everything if you sell less than twenty-five thousand dollars a year. American law doesn't care about the small producer.

I'm sure I'm in the right because I've studied my state's laws, talked to lawyers, and done thorough research. I advise you to do the same. But I also have to say that since I've been doing this work, I've never had a restaurant tell me to show them my license or show them that it's legal for me to sell them this product; they are just happy to get my product.

Is this business right for you?

So first, you need to find out if growing and selling microgreens is profitable in your area. And also, whether you are the correct type of person to succeed in a microgreens business.

Starting a business is not for everyone. You may not be in a stage of life right now where you can devote the time and energy to get your microgreens business off the ground.

MICROGREENS BUSINESS

If you can't fully commit to your business, it may be best to wait for a better time before you start.

Getting started in microgreens production allows you to enter new markets and expand existing markets. The ability to grow these micro-vegetables in a small space and on vertical shelves allows for an exciting production idea.

FINDING YOUR NICHE

One of the most critical decisions in starting a business is to understand what you want to sell. As mentioned earlier, not all markets are the same. First, you need to understand what product consumers in your area need most. Next, you need to try to find your niche.

Generally, those who sell microgreens follow one of the following three strategies:

1. Mainly sell commodity microgreens such as radishes, peas, sunflowers, brassicas.
2. Mainly sell specialty microgreens such as beets, corn shoots, cilantro, basil, mustard, amaranth, etc.
3. Sell all varieties.

You almost certainly won't be able to sell all varieties initially, but you'll need to choose one of the other two solutions. If there are no other microgreens sellers in your local market, you can quickly start with commodity microgreens, which are easier to sell because they are better known.

Conversely, if there are already other sellers in your market, try selling microgreens varieties they don't have and focus more on specialty products.

The good news is that the growth rate of these products allows you to change your offering quickly. So, if at any point you find that one product is more in demand than another, you can start producing it immediately.

The best microgreens to grow

Microgreens come in a wide variety of shapes, colours (green, yellow, red, purple), textures (tender, crunchy, juicy), and flavours (sweet, neutral, sour, spicy) offered by the different varieties.

Radishes, broccoli, arugula and cabbage are among the easiest species to grow. Sunflower microgreens are also very popular and are among the most commercially viable. However, the latter pose a few more problems for beginners. For more information, I recommend that you read the last section of this book, which contains detailed information about the main types of microgreens you might want to grow and sell.

MICROGREENS BUSINESS

The advice I can give you to get started is to focus on a few varieties of microgreens. You can begin by growing just three or four types. Over time, you can decide to expand your production to other varieties as well.

MICROGREENS BUSINESS

GROWING MICROGREENS

As mentioned earlier, microgreens can be grown in two ways: in soil or hydroponically. Growing in soil is more straightforward and suitable for beginners. In the following sections, I will show you both ways.

You will definitely need to buy seeds that have been explicitly produced and packaged for micro-greens. These seeds have low levels of foreign matter, are not treated with fungicides or other chemicals, and are well cleaned.

This is especially important when buying seeds for pea, corn, or spinach microgreens, as these species' seeds are usually treated with a fungicide. Seed companies have also introduced several special microgreens varieties that are a marked improvement over the standard types.

Many of these have brightly colored or modified first leaves, such as green-leaved radish varieties and those bred for pea shoots. Some microgreen varieties have mucilaginous seeds, which means the seeds form a thick, gelatinous layer that retains the moisture once moistened.

Watercress and basil are examples of mucilaginous seeds, and you should not soak these types of seeds before sowing. Larger grains such as wheatgrass, corn, and peas can be soaked in warm water 24 hours before sowing, although this step is not essential.

The microgreen seed should then be weighed and sown as evenly as possible on the wet surface - the use of seed shakers will help. The correct seeding density depends somewhat on the species being cultivated.

Once the seeds have germinated, microgreens need light and nutrients to produce a high-quality product. Artificial lighting does not need to be intense, and these young seedlings do well under grow lights as long as the lights do not produce too much heat that can burn the tender young foliage.

When the cotyledons (seedling leaves) are visible and begin to develop chlorophyll, the seedlings have used up the reserves contained in the seed. At this stage, the young plant begins to photosynthesize and produce its own assimilates, and the root system takes up nutrient ions.

Generally, after about ten days after sowing (it may be more or less, depending on the variety you grow), you can start harvesting.

However, before choosing a method (with or without soil), you need to understand which is ideal for the seeds you want to grow.

Soil Method: step by step instructions

To grow your microgreens using this method, first make sure you have all the material you need:

- Seeds
- Water jar
- Growing trays with drainage holes
- Growing trays without drainage holes
- Soil mix
- Spray bottle

You can buy all of these materials individually at specialty stores or, even better, in special kits that include everything you need. If you want to save money, you can buy the seeds and use the materials you already have in the house.

Below are general instructions that you can use for most

seeds that can be grown in soil. However, certain microgreens may require special care. It is therefore always advisable to read the instructions that the seed supplier usually includes with the products. The best suppliers can also give advice and explain everything you need to do to grow these specific seeds that you have purchased.

Step 1: soaking

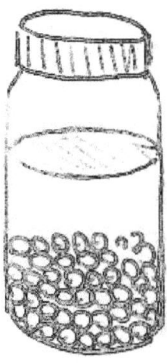

Wash the seeds with a filter, germination bag, or in a germination container.

Soak the seeds for about 4-8 hours (depending on the size of the grain). You can soak them in the same bag or jar.

Place the seeds in the germination bag or jar and wait for them to germinate. You will need to wash them two or three times a day. Once they reach the same size as the grain, they are ready for sowing.

You can skip the previous two steps and sow the seeds directly on the moist substrate, especially if they are very small or slimy seeds.

Step 2: preparing the grow tray

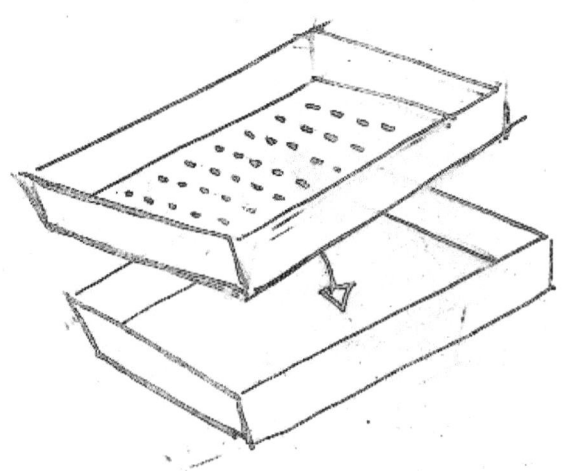

Insert the planting tray (with holes) into the watering tray (without holes). Prepare the growing tray by spreading the substrate on the tray with drainage holes, forming a 2-3 cm thick layer. You can use containers that you have at home or special trays made for this purpose.

Ensure that there are no pieces of wood or other materials in the soil that would hinder the growth of plants. Then press lightly on the soil with your hand to smooth it out. You can use a spatula to help you do this. Do not overdo the pressure: the soil should not be too compact.

Soak the soil with water without puddling it to keep it moist and spongy.

Step 3: planting

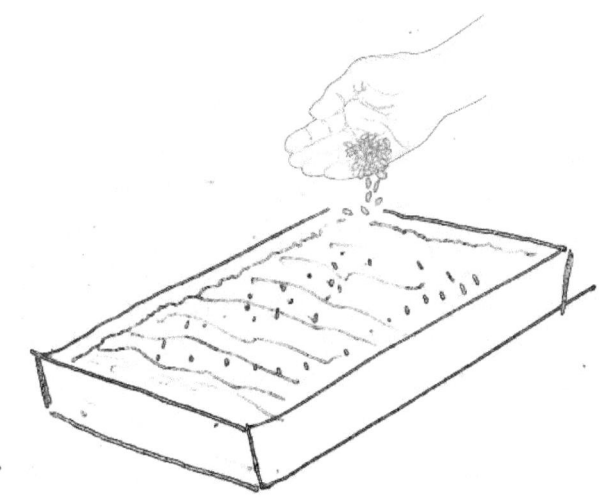

Spread the germinated or ungerminated seeds evenly over the ground and compact them a little with your hands. You should leave enough space between each seed. This space can vary depending on the size of the seed. As a rule of thumb, space should be the same size as the seed you are planting.

Step 4: covering

Cover the seeds with a light layer of soil and water them lightly with your spray bottle (this will encourage germination). Now take the tray without holes, spray some water into it (this will create a humid indoor environment) and then cover the first tray. You can now put the tray in a place that is not too hot or too cold.

Step 5: maintenance

Every 12 hours, lift the lid and spray some water to keep the soil moist. It is essential to keep the soil moist without letting it puddle, do not let it dry out.

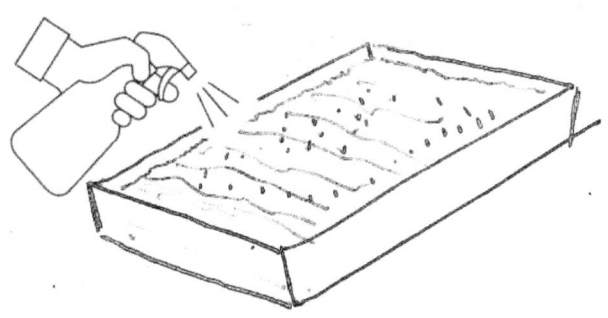

At this stage, the plants can be enriched with a solution based on compounds rich in trace elements, increasing the nutritional value of the plant, but this is entirely optional. Two options for fertilizing our micro garden are kelp type algae powder or macerated compost.

MICROGREENS BUSINESS

Step 6: uncovering

During the first 3-4 days, you must keep the plant in the dark (the "blackout period"). After this time, the tiny leaves of your plant will appear.

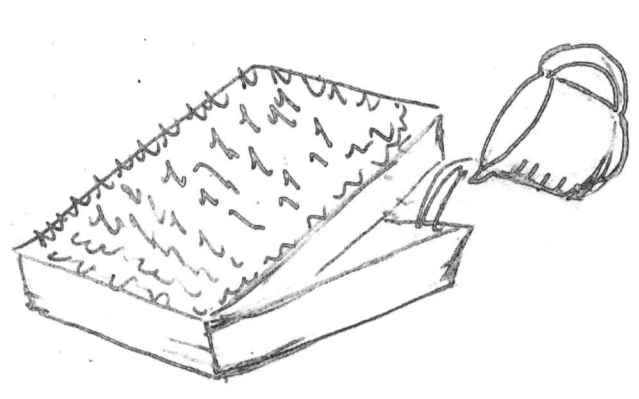

Now you can lift the upper tray (the one with holes) and pour some water into the lower tray (the one without holes). This way, your seedlings can absorb the water not only through the upper mist but also through the roots.

Step 7: growing

Microgreens need much light. Therefore, it is necessary to expose them to direct sunlight after 3-5 days or, even better, use LED lamps.

At this stage, it is crucial to keep the plants well hydrated. The soil needs to be moist but not soggy. Check regularly, including weighing the tray (if the soil is too dry, the tray will be very light).

Step 8: harvesting

After 2 -4 weeks after sowing, your microgreens will reach the desired size. Now you can gather them by hand with scissors or a sharp knife in small bunches, from the outside inwards and at ground level.

Cutting height is critical because high-quality microgreens require a good, clean portion of the stem below the leaves, but they should not be cut so low as to risk contamination with the growing medium or material in which the seeds were sown.

This is especially important if a light, granular medium was used for production, as particles can be easily trapped during the harvesting process and contaminate the product. Clean, sharp shears are suitable for cutting microgreens on a small scale, while larger growers use mechanical harvesters.

During warm growing climates, microgreens, like herbs and lettuce, are best harvested earlier in the day when the foliage is still cooler and plumper. This extends the life of the packaged product.

Please note: Do not throw away the soil after harvesting. You can still use it to make compost!

Step 9: Storing

After harvesting, you need to dry the microgreens. You can use a sieve to do this and then use some paper towels. When the microgreens are completely dry, you can store them in the refrigerator for a few days.

Some microgreens are shipped to customers while still growing in trays or cells to extend shelf life and be harvested on-site when needed.

Hydroponic method

Hydroponics consists of the cultivation of various species without the use of soil. Contrary to what many people think, it is not expensive to do hydroponics at home. There are hydroponic systems on the market that are designed for small spaces and at an affordable price.

Hydroponic microgreens have a distinct advantage over those grown in substrate trays or soil mixes because there is no granular growing medium to use. The high seeding rate and density of microgreens mean that tiny particles of the substrate can get into the foliage. Since microgreens are not usually washed off after harvest, there is a risk of the crunchy grains getting into the final dish.

For this reason, hydroponic microgreens are best grown in a thin or capillary mat that holds the seed in place and retains some moisture for germination. Paper towels, linen cloths, rock wool cubes or sheets, fine kitchen towels, and hydroponic microgreens pads can all be used to grow a clean, high-quality crop at a low cost.

Hydroponic systems for microgreens can be as simple as a small, flat, hand-irrigated kitchen tray or as complex as a nutrient or aeroponic film technology system. Ideally, the growing system needs to have a balanced, slightly sloped surface to lay out and moisten the ever-growing mat/pillow paper or fabric.

MICROGREENS BUSINESS

Doing hydroponics at home is very easy; you can buy your hydroponic system or build it at home. Hydroponics is an excellent form of growing; with this technique, you can grow lettuce, arugula, herbs, kohlrabi, cabbage, strawberries, tomatoes, among others, in a small and compact space. You can do this growing at home, in your apartment, in the kitchen or even on the terrace.

These hydroponic kits allow you to cultivate about 40 to 90 plants per month and can be used for lettuce, arugula, herbs, beets, cabbage, strawberries, tomatoes, among others. The time from cultivation to harvest varies depending on the species grown..

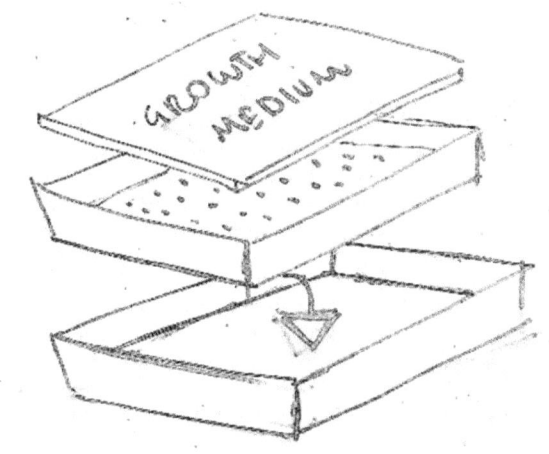

From a practical point of view, the steps for growing microgreens hydroponically are no different from those already described for the soil method. The seeds used are the same as those used in traditional cultivation. You still need a planting tray and a watering tray.

In this case, the only difference is that you do not plant the seeds in soil but another growing medium such as phenolic foam, coconut fiber, rock wool, or vermiculite.

I recommend phenolic foam as it is more practical, hygienic and biodegradable. It provides good support for the tiny seedlings and is porous so that the roots are optimally supplied with moisture..

Will microgreens regrow?

Unfortunately, most microgreens do not grow back after harvest. This is because microgreens have only one set of leaves. After harvest, the plants can no longer absorb the sun's rays and therefore die. A few exceptions to this rule: microgreen shoots, such as peas, beans, and lentils, may regrow a few times. After harvesting, if the stems continue to be watered, sometimes a second plant will resprout.

However, when they do regrow, they lose some of their flavour. Therefore, it is not recommended to reuse the same plants if you are growing microgreens for commercial purposes. Finally, the cost of the seeds is so low compared to what you can get from selling the seedlings that it is worth planting new microgreens every time.

COMMON PROBLEMS (AND HOW TO SOLVE THEM)

As we have seen, microgreens are an ideal crop for small indoor gardeners. They are fast, productive, and with only a few inches of well-lit space - they can be grown quickly on a warm, sunny windowsill or incorporated into a high-tech hydroponic system. Their short shelf life makes them a good candidate for local markets and restaurants, as they are best used within two to three days of harvest.

However, it takes some skill to cultivate these seedlings at high densities and maintain quality after harvest, and some problems may arise during operations.

Clumpy microgreens

I already told you that an essential part of growing your microgreens is planting the seeds, which you must adequately space in the trays. You need to leave the right amount of space between each seed. Unfortunately, it can be challenging to get an even distribution, and this can lead to problems. If the roots are too close together, they can clump together. This problem is even more significant with mucilaginous seeds.

The problem occurs when the plants sprout because if you haven't left enough space, one plant could uproot the other. Not only can this bring dirt, but it can also make harvesting difficult. In addition, the plants that emerge from these clumped seeds are often very inconsistent in growth.

When sowing slime seeds, you should take extra care to distribute the seeds evenly in the tray. In some cases, it is advisable to reduce the number of seeds per tray to avoid seed clumping.

Uneven growth

Sometimes microgreens may not grow evenly across the tray. For example, you may have well-grown plants on one side of the tray and much shorter ones on another side of the tray.

A lack of light usually causes this problem. Seedlings naturally grow better in the part of the tray where there is more light, and worse where there is less light. This problem can occur especially if you are not using LED lights (which illuminate the entire tray evenly). Limited sunlight can cause one area to grow better and taller than another. You will need to provide artificial light to the shorter side or rotate the trays regularly so that light falls on all the microgreens.

Mold

Several fungal pathogens can develop and grow in germinated seeds, especially in the moist, high-density conditions in which microgreens are grown, and this can pose a contamination risk.

Mold is one of the main problems you may face when growing your microgreens. Before you understand how to combat it, you need to be able to recognize it. First, you need to be able to distinguish mold from root hairs. White, fuzzy hairs grow on the roots of microgreens, but they are not mold. Mold is a fungus that comes in a variety of forms. Mold on microgreens appears as a net-like material that is typically white or yellow. Some types of mold are blue/gray with round particles.

Mold feels slimy and has a characteristic odor. It can form on the microgreens, on the soil around the microgreens, and sometimes underground on the roots.

Mold kills or stops the growth of microgreens. However, it is a problem that you can solve.

Generally, high quality, viable seeds, sown in a clean system at the right temperature for germination and optimum moisture germinate quickly with few problems.

If you find that the soil you grew the microgreens is contaminated with mold, you can transplant them into new soil, which almost always solves the problem.

To prevent mold even before it forms, you can disinfect the seeds. Some growers use this with hydrogen peroxide. This chemical removes all bacteria from the seeds and ensures that there are not many complications.

Generally, however, it is enough to give the plants proper hydration, lighting and ventilation, and you will not have problems with mold or fungus.

Fungus

Microgreens, like all plants, can be susceptible to disease and can be attacked by fungi. The biggest threat to microgreens seems to be Pythium and Phytophthora, two common fungal species that also attack other plant species. The main difference between Pythium and

Phytophthora are their symptoms. Root rot, slow growth, stunting and chlorotic foliage are symptoms of Pythium disease, while root and stem rot, discoloration and wilting are symptoms of Phytophthora disease.

These fungi affect plants, but at the root of the problem are the same things that cause mold: little space between seeds and no air circulation.

The best practices gardeners can use to prevent disease are to pay attention to temperature, humidity, growing medium selection and spacing. Because the growth cycle is so short with microgreens, the seedlings themselves are not treated with pesticides. Disease outbreaks are more common when old seeds are used or temperatures are too hot or cold for rapid germination. Some varieties of microgreens such as chard, Thai basil, mint and nasturtium are more susceptible to disease and insect problems.

Slow germination

When you're growing microgreens, sometimes you think you've taken care of everything. Then suddenly, you find that your plant has stopped growing or is growing slowly. Since microgreens are harvested very early, you should see germination within two to four days. Although some seeds may take a little longer, something is most likely wrong if you notice a noticeable increase in time.

To speed up the germination process, try increasing the humidity in the tray. If you notice that the soil is drying out, it means that you should spray the tray more often.

Be careful though, too much water can be a problem too!

Also, pay attention to the seeds you use - old or low-quality seeds are a common cause of all kinds of growing problems. If you use bad seeds, your plants may be slow to grow, stunted, or fail to germinate. For best results, choose only quality seeds that you buy from reputable suppliers.

Also, pay attention to lighting: your microgreens love and need plenty of light, but too much is not good. Direct and constant exposure to intense sunlight or high-intensity indoor lighting can stress your plants and lead to slow growth and other problems. If you are growing indoors and think too much light is the cause of your problem, keep the plants further away from the light to reduce its intensity.

Bad quality water

As a small microgreens producer, you've probably compared the results of different soils or different temperatures or different types of lighting. Still, you probably haven't considered that the kind of water you use also has an impact.

The water supply needs to be of high quality. Water can contain human and plant pathogens that contaminate a crop. However, municipal water supplies are treated to avoid this risk.

One could think of performing different types of water analysis (municipal tap water or bottled spring water or collected rainwater or well water) in a laboratory, but this would be not only impractical but also expensive. It is best to judge the quality of the water by the results. And your results are the microgreens.

Grow two lots of seeds in the same soil under identical light, darkness and heat, but not water. For example, you get two collections: one with bottled water and the other with tap water. Do they look the same after two weeks? If not, the microgreens washed with tap water are slightly yellow, but the other batch is not, then chlorine is to blame.

The chlorine in tap water helps to eliminate bacteria but can hurt plants. If you find that your water contains too much chlorine, you can put it in containers and let it sit for a day without buying it. Chlorine is a volatile substance and evaporates quickly, making the water better for your plants.

Also, pay attention to lighting: your microgreens love and need plenty of light, but too much is not good. Direct and constant exposure to intense sunlight or high-intensity indoor lighting can stress your plants and lead to slow growth and other problems. If you are growing indoors and think too much light is the cause of your problem, keep the plants further away from the light to reduce its intensity.

Overwatering

One of the most common problems observed in microgreens production is seedling blight and disease outbreaks caused by too much water or high humidity, creating a saturated environment around the foliage.

Too much water or high humidity can cause mold to grow on microgreens. So first of all, you must avoid giving your plants too much water at all costs. In any case, I recommend that you also use systems that facilitate water drainage and eliminate the problem of moisture in the soil. First, as we have already seen, it is advisable to use trays with holes in the bottom through which the water not absorbed by the plants can drain.

Secondly, it is advisable to use a soil that facilitates drainage. For example, peat moss or coconut fiber helps to improve airflow in the soil.

Poor ventilation

We often take air for granted (perhaps because we can't

see it or touch it). Yet air is essential to our survival. If there were none, we could not breathe and would die. The same is true for the plants we grow.

Plants need air and even a little wind. This serves to help them grow more naturally and become strong.

Ventilation is a mechanical method of providing fresh air, and plants need fresh air no less than you do. Unfortunately, a windowless garage will not have adequate ventilation to ensure good plant growth. For this reason, it is advisable (as I will show you later) to install small fans near the plants to provide good air movement and to avoid problems with root rot, fungal and bacterial pathogens.

The room where you grow microgreens will have a fresh scent, and the environment will be healthier both day and night.

Plants keep falling over

Microgreens can grow too tall and fall over, making harvesting extremely difficult. In addition, when microgreens grow too tall, they tend to become thin and flabby and therefore fall off easily.

Therefore, you should prune this crop at the right time.

To avoid weak microgreens, you also need to pay attention to lighting and especially to the blackout period, which is the time you keep the microgreens covered and in the dark after sowing.

The blackout period for microgreens lasts as long as necessary for the seeds to germinate, root deeply, and grow to a point where they are ready to begin photosynthesis.

The longer microgreens are kept in the dark, the thinner and lighter they become. If you forget to take them out, there is a length limit in which they can grow. Therefore, you need to time the darkening period correctly.

There are many variables to consider, such as:

- The microgreen variety;
- soil and air temperatures;
- Moisture level.

Generally, you should check the seeds after 48 hours to see how well they have germinated and their growth stage. For some varieties like radishes, beets, mustard, broccoli and kohlrabi, 48 hours is long enough. For other types like cilantro, celery, borage and others, the cutoff time can be four to six days.

HYGIENE AND FOOD SAFETY REGULATIONS

The sale of microgreens, like any other food, is subject to specific regulations.

There are growing concerns and more regulations regarding food safety, so commercial growers of microgreens need to know the guidelines they must follow for fresh produce food safety.

Identify the laws in your area

So, if you want to get into this business, it's good to study the laws first. Of course, regulations vary from country to country, but even within a country, they can differ. In the U.S., for example, you may find yourself in a city, county, or township that has zoning regulations. In this case, you need to check if commercial farming is allowed in your neighborhood. You can find out by going to your planning and building department, which may be called something different in your county. Your best bet is to go to the county courthouse or city clerk's office, find a clerk or receptionist, and tell them you have a question about zoning.

Generally, in the U.S., the Department of Agriculture in each state administers licenses to sell raw agricultural products. You do not need a license in many states if you only sell products from your farm or garden (and your garage is a farm). Licensing is only required if you buy produce from others and resell it or if you add ingredients to your microgreens that are not from your farm.

Food Safety Modernization Act

In theory, microgreens fall under the Food Safety Modernization Act (FSMA). This regulation establishes requirements for a written food safety plan, hazard analysis, preventive controls, monitoring, corrective actions and corrections, verification, a supply chain program, a recall plan, and related records. However, there is one important exception: if your sales are less than $25,000 per year, you do not have to comply with this requirement.

But even if you sell up to $500,000 a year directly to "qualified end users," including grocery stores and restaurants, you have a partial exemption.

In any case, I have to say that the food safety protocols required by FSMA are things that all farms should continue to do to protect themselves from foodborne illness: Basic sanitation, taking steps to prevent animals like mice and birds from pooping on the product, hand washing by workers who collect and handle the product, cleaning and sanitizing food contact surfaces like wash tables and packing containers, testing the water if it is not from an already tested municipal water system.

Good Agricultural Practices

There are some certification programs you can take voluntarily, even if they are not required by law. Your customers will likely be interested in your on-farm food safety measures. They might ask you if you have a GAP audit. This type of certification is also advantageous from a marketing perspective because if buyers are familiar with something, it's probably GAPs. Good Agricultural

MICROGREENS BUSINESS

Practices (GAPs) are voluntary guidelines for farmers to reduce the risk of microbial contamination associated with foodborne illness on their farms. The guidelines are based on the Food and Drug Administration (FDA) guidance at Minimizing Microbial Food Safety Hazards for Fresh Produce. This is probably the most common certification you can get as a small farmer.

Your state's Department of Agriculture conducts GAP audits, and there is a fee. Farmers must pay for GAP audits. Some states, such as Minnesota, have a cost-share program for GAP certification. If you choose to go this route, you can receive a 75% reimbursement for the cost of the GAP audit.

If you choose to do this audit, the Department of Agriculture will send staff to your location to do the inspections. They will inspect your farm to make sure you have good refrigeration, an excellent wash station, that you keep your area clean, that you clean your trays, that you sanitize things, that you don't use rusty old knives for harvesting, that you wash them every time and other things like that.

I know the fact of undergoing inspections might be intimidating to you. Still, I also have to say that as long as you follow good practices as you would in your kitchen (you safely handle food, like you would if you were eating it yourself), you usually won't have any problems.

MICROGREENS BUSINESS

Having this kind of certification, while not mandatory, can be very useful, both to have greater personal peace of mind and to better sell your microgreens..

MICROGREENS BUSINESS

HOW TO SET UP A SMALL VERTICAL FARM

The great thing about microgreens is that you can develop a large growing area vertically in a small space. So if you have an empty room in your house or a closet or garage, you can certainly think of using it for this activity. In any case, you will need some shelving system or vertical growing rack.

With a vertical growing rack, you can grow more microgreens and use less space and water. As a result, you can save energy, optimize space, improve safety, and maximize profits.

Particular grow racks for growing microgreens are

available at specialty stores. Most of them are great, and if you have a reasonable budget, I recommend buying them.

Microgreen Rack

The problem is that the price of a professional microgreens grow rack can quickly go over $1,000 or even $2,000 (like the one shown in the picture). You may not have that kind of money, but don't worry, the solution exists. You don't need any special equipment or investment to build an indoor grow rack.

With chrome wire shelves, indoor grow lights, and fans, you can safely build microgreens grow rack in your home. For easy setup, you can find everything you need on Amazon.

Shelving system

The first thing you need to build your microgreens grow rack is a shelving system on which you will place the trays containing your plants.

You don't necessarily have to buy shelves that are designed for growing microgreens. Instead, you can use the same frames that are used for closets, garages, or offices.

Chromed wire shelving is better than sheet metal shelving because it allows for better transpiration between tiers.

For example, a 48 x 72 x 24-inch four-tier shelf costs only about sixty dollars if you buy it on Amazon.

Led Grow Lights

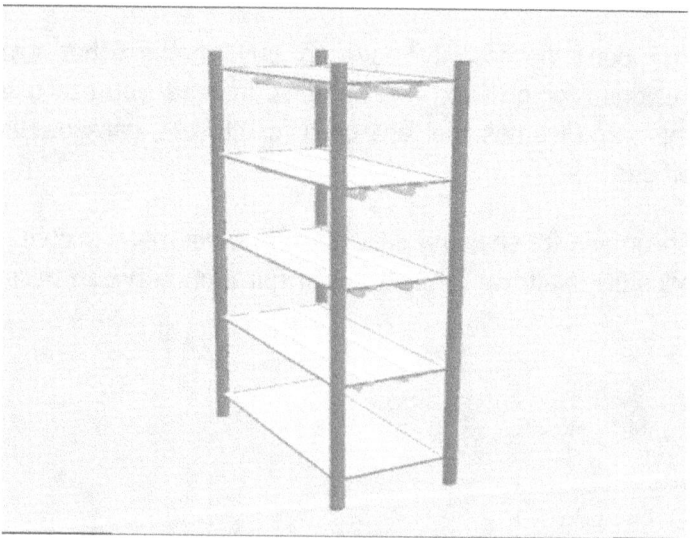

The second thing you will need to build your professional grow rack is lighting. In this case, I recommend buying LED grow lights. LED grow lights provide indoor plants with full-spectrum sunlight replacement. It is a perfect option for growing microgreens.

There are all kinds of them on Amazon. For example, a package of 8 LED grow light costs only $60 and includes 8 X 10 WATT grow lights with everything you need to assemble them.

MICROGREENS BUSINESS

You can install the lights yourself in minutes. Plug in the 10-watt lights with the included power cords with triangular plugs to hold them firmly to the ceiling of any shelf without cable ties.

USB fans

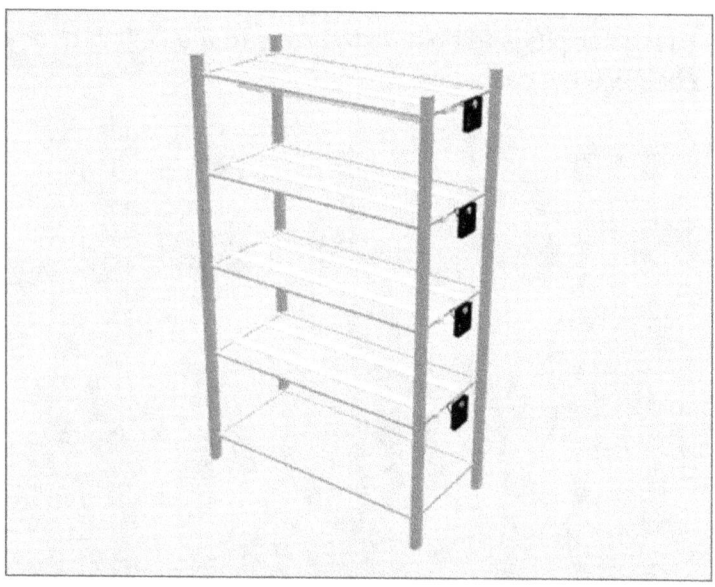

Microgreens can easily grow in a windowless room, but you need to provide the seedlings with some air for the best results. For this purpose, commercial racks have built-in fans. These are used to properly aerate microgreens, as they need air between the leaves to grow.

You can quickly solve the problem by getting cheap fans. I recommend you buy the same USB fans that are used for PC cases. They are very economical, quiet, and usually have three speeds. The price for a USB fan is about $10, and you will need one for each shelf. You can find a lot of them on Amazon.

MICROGREENS BUSINESS

You can attach them to the shelves with zip ties and plug them into a USB outlet.

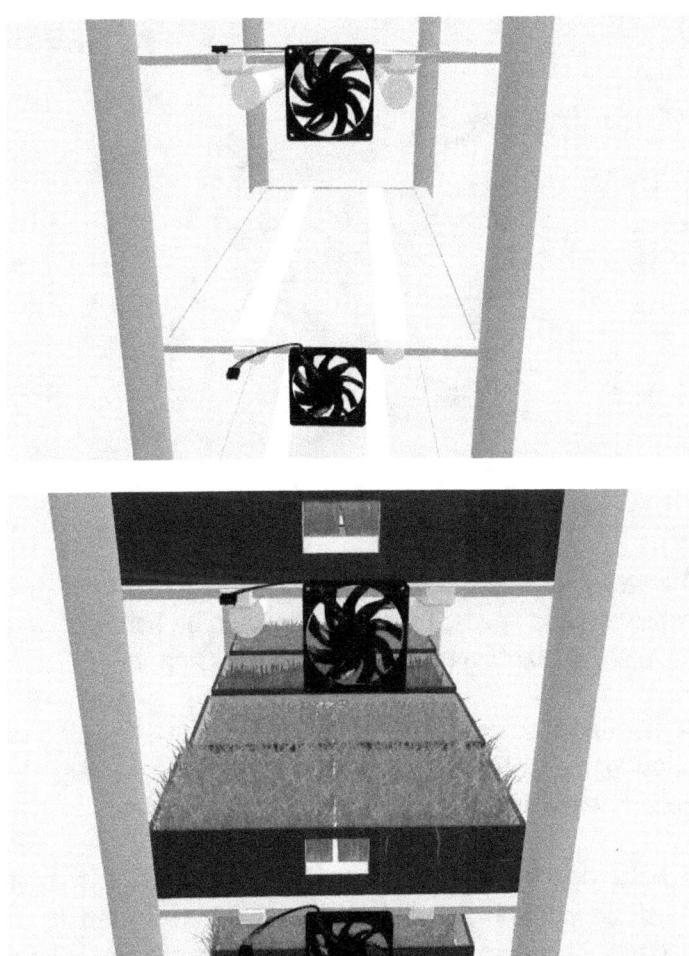

Microgreen trays

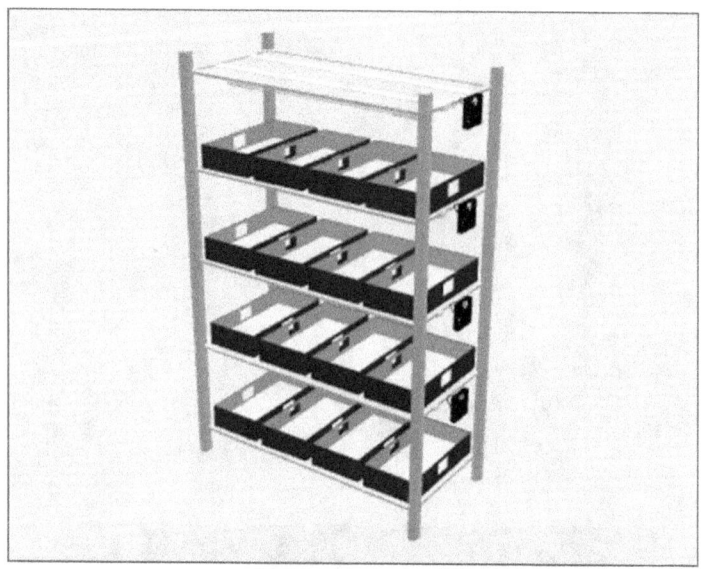

As we've already seen, trays are used to house the substrate and seeds. Therefore, it would be helpful if you have some planting trays and some watering trays.

A planting tray or container needs to have soil holes to allow extra water to drain through and large enough to absorb water into the soil medium when it is dry.

A watering tray must be larger than the planting tray, or it must be possible to slide the planting tray into it. In addition, of course, the watering tray must be solid to hold water, and the sides must be high enough so that water does not overflow when the planters are placed in the watering tray.

The standard size for trays is 10 x 20 inches, and the price is about $3 each. You can put up to 16 trays on a shelf with four compartments, as the one described. That means you should buy 16 planting trays and 16 watering trays for a total cost of about $96 (=32 x $3). Microgreens trays are reusable, so you only have to pay this cost once.

Cost estimates

In summary, building a grow rack like the one described would cost you about:

- 1 Chrome Wire Shelf: $ 60

- 8 Led Grow lights: $ 60
- 4 USB fans: $ 40
- 16 watering trays: $ 48
- 16 planting trays: $ 48

TOTAL COST: $ 256.

Profit estimates

If you put together two or more grow racks like the one described in the previous section, you can build your vertical farm.

To understand how much you can benefit, I suggest you start asking yourself these questions:

- How many trays of microgreens can you put in a grow rack?
- How many grow racks can you put in your space?
- How much production would you have in a month?

For example, let's say you use the same rack described in the previous section (48" x 72" x 24").

As we have seen, you could fit twenty 10x20 trays in this rack.

In a 60-square-foot room, you could easily put four racks. You would then come up with a total of 64 10x20 trays.

MICROGREENS BUSINESS

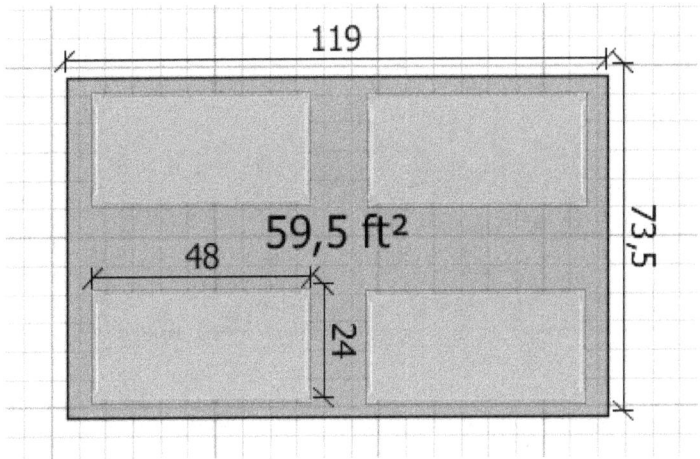

The production cycle of microgreens averages two weeks, so your production capacity would be 128 trays per month.

We said that the average retail price for a tray of microgreens is between $12.5 and $18.8. This means that the monthly production value of a growing system like the one we just described is between $1600 (= $12.5 x 128) and $2406 (= $18.8 x 128).

That's not bad at all, especially considering you could put more grow racks in a slightly larger space and increase production exponentially. To give you an example, in a 70-square-foot room, you could quickly put six racks. You would then come up with a total of 96 trays, a production capacity of 192 trays per month and a production value between $2400 (=$12.5 x 192) and $3609 (= $18,8 x 192).

MICROGREENS BUSINESS

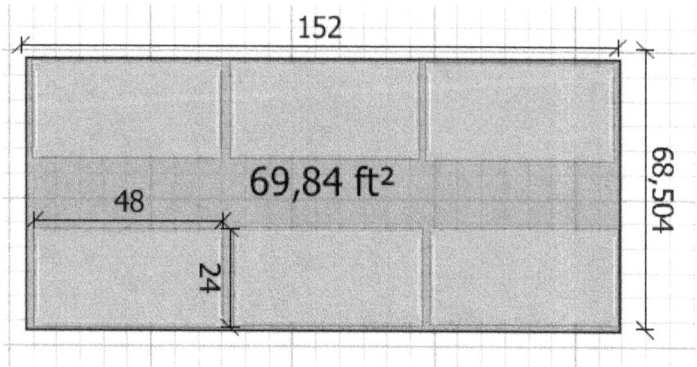

To understand how much you would earn, you must also consider the costs associated with producing microgreens. These costs (aside from the fixed costs of the grow racks) are for the trays, seeds, soil, electricity, water, and labor. A detailed estimate of all these costs would take too long now, but you can reasonably assume an average cost per tray of about $4. That brings your monthly cost to $768 (= $4 x 192). So, if you include these costs as well, you could end up with a net margin of between $1632 (=$2400-$778) and $2841 (=$3609 − $768)

Now consider that some microgreens, such as broccoli or sunflower, grow much faster than others. If you decided to grow only these, your monthly production capacity would double, giving you 384 trays per month. Your potential monthly profit would range from $4800 (= $12.5 x 384) to $7219 (= $18.8 x 384). Your monthly variable production costs would be $1526 (= $4 x 384). Ultimately, your net profit margin would be between $3264 (= $4800 − $1526) and $5693 (= $7219 − $1526).

MICROGREENS BUSINESS

MICROGREENS BUSINESS

MARKETING MICROGREENS

Now that you know what microgreens are and how to grow them, it's time to think about marketing. Selling the product may not be your problem if your only goal is to grow your microgreens for your own use. However, since you bought this book, I suspect that you also want to start your own business.

To succeed as a professional microgreen grower, it's not enough that you're simply good at growing your seedlings. You will inevitably need to do some calculating, you will need to understand something about taxes, and most importantly, you will need to learn a little about marketing.

Let's say your business is the only one selling microgreens within a 200 km radius.

MICROGREENS BUSINESS

In this scenario, the consumer looking for microgreens would be forced to take the car and come to you to buy the product. He would not ask many questions about the price, quality, variety, etc., and he would definitely buy your microgreens for sale. You would not have many other worries besides growing your microgreens.

In some areas, the situation you are in is really similar to the one described because microgreens are still a very new product.

Unfortunately, there are also areas where things are pretty different.

As competition increases, so does the price war and the exploitation of advertising.

So why should consumers choose your microgreens over what others offer? It would be best if you used specific strategies to convince the customer to buy from you.

Nowadays, it is not enough to produce an excellent product; you must also communicate by creating a dialog that can engage the customer.

This is even more true because a small business like yours will never win the price war with big retailers.

You need to do marketing, and your marketing strategy should consist of several components that help consumers understand why they should buy your product and not another.

My microgreens are so good, but no one knows it

Many farmers feel forced to sell to wholesalers at inadequate prices. Many growers act only as producers, not traders or specialized sellers, so their primary obligation is to produce excellent products.

They think that's the farmer's job consist of producing an excellent product. And they do that.

The problem is that it is not enough to know how to make good products in today's world. You also need to understand how to sell them.

It is the fundamental difference between the quality of the product (how good are the microgreens) and the quality perceived by the market (microgreens are good, but do your customers know that?).

Your microgreens can be the best on the market, but the consumer needs to know, and this is where marketing comes in, which is an entirely different field than microgreens production.

It doesn't matter if your microgreens are 100% organic,

good for your health, reduce cancer risk and so on. You need to have a marketing strategy that uses the proper channels to get that message out!

They can be very fresh products and therefore full of nutrients. They can have been grown without chemicals, but the consumer does not have an analytical laboratory at home and therefore must believe in a promotional message that explains the quality of the products.

In summary, you need to be fully aware of your strengths and then launch a solid marketing campaign.

Indeed, it is useless to produce quality products if no one knows it. And it is marketing that bridges this gap.

A microgreen producer must spend a large portion of his budget on marketing, which is often not the case because the producer focuses solely on producing quality products.

Generally, the average consumer does not recognize the difference between a microgreen and another type of product, often dwells on the price. The average consumer sometimes does not understand why he should pay $3 for an ounce of microgreen onions when he could buy ordinary onions at a lower price.

Sometimes consumer cannot see the value of microgreens for himself because he doesn't know what they are. For this reason, it is crucial to make him aware that his choice of this product is essential not only to his palate but also to his health.

And this is where a professional marketing plan must come into play to educate the consumer by showing them the strengths of microgreens.

The importance of marketing planning

We have seen why the microgreens entrepreneur needs to invest in marketing, but how do you do it?

Thinking about your entrepreneurial work from a marketing perspective means asking yourself a whole series of practical questions and then harmonizing them into a global strategy. When thinking about your agricultural work in promotional terms, you need to:

- Know your current strengths and use them.
- Also, understand your weaknesses and know if and how you can develop methods to overcome them.
- Study the market around you and analyze the needs to be met.

In the microgreens sector, it is possible to become a reference in terms of quality in a local area, but this does not mean that a strong marketing effort is not required.

Marketing is based on analysis, ideas, even intuitions. Still, it must not be improvised: It requires a strategic plan with actions to be implemented, with precise, measurable and repeatable times and costs.

A simple, intuitive plan that can be modified and analyzed over time.

Without planning, you waste time and money: marketing for microgreens must be done professionally.

Marketing planning means understanding where and how to distribute the product (whom to sell it to), how to promote it, how to create a recognizable brand image, and how to price it. Don't worry: I'll tell you about all of these things in the following few paragraphs.

DISTRIBUTION

One of the first things you need to understand is where to sell your products. Your business will be a small business with a small, high-quality home production. Large scale retail will not be your preferred distribution channel. Large retailers usually want to be supplied by large producers who can supply large quantities of products at low prices.

Similarly, we tend to rule out the possibility that you will want to sell your micro-vegetables overseas. It is certainly possible (and some producers do) to export your micro vegetables to markets where prices to the end consumer are much higher than where you live locally. Still, it is a difficult road to travel. In all likelihood, you would be up against large producers, and you would not stop the competition. For these reasons, the best way to distribute your microgreens is through the local market. But even in this case, you need to know that every market is different, and therefore you need to study your particular market well before making your choice.

Where to sell microgreens

The main distribution channels are basically four: restaurants, grocery stores, direct sales and farmers markets.

Restaurants

Restaurants are a great distribution channel for your microgreens. Especially if you live in a medium or large city, you can find many good customers in your area. Many chefs use microgreens because they are a very fresh produce with a unique flavor. In addition, many restaurant owners prefer to buy their raw ingredients from small local suppliers rather than big retailers, even if they have to pay a little more. This way, restaurants can tell their customers that they are using only natural products locally grown and not contaminated by chemical fertilizers and preservatives (often used in industrial production). Also, your product will always be fresher than what you can buy in big retail stores (if there are any) and have a longer shelf life. As a result, restaurants will happily pay a higher price for these products as they charge their customers a price that reflects the high quality of what they offer.

Since not all restaurants are the same, you may be wondering what type of restaurant is best to offer your microgreens. It's not an easy question to answer, as things can differ from one area to another. I certainly don't recommend going to McDonald's to offer your products, but it's also not necessarily the case that you should only provide your microgreens at high-end restaurants. You could easily find many small restaurants that aren't overly luxurious, but carefully select the raw ingredients they buy and might be interested in your offering.

So for starting, I suggest you take a tour of the restaurants in your area and bring a price list and any marketing information materials you can show to prospects. It would also be a good idea to get some free, possibly well packaged, small samples of your microgreens. That way, the restaurateurs can sample the product and see for themselves how good it is. I assure you that this is a great way to convince the customer.

Don't worry if you don't get much success at first. For a business like yours, it is not necessary to have many customers. Instead, you need a few good restaurant customers to break even. I know several small microgreen producers who manage to net $3,000 a week by targeting restaurants in their area.

MICROGREENS BUSINESS

Grocery stores

Grocery stores, like restaurants, can be an excellent outlet for your products.

The principle of "smaller is better" applies to them as well. Mini-markets and corner shops are traditionally more interested in quality and less price-sensitive than supermarkets. The owners of these stores like to source their goods from small local producers because they care about quality and always want fresh produce, which is not always possible.

If you want to have this kind of customer, you need to personally introduce yourself to the shop owners and tell them about your products, how they are made and what benefits they bring. To this end, it is handy if you have product samples with you that you can give to the owner to test. Ideally, these products should already be packaged for sale. Since you will almost certainly meet people who don't know microgreens at all, I recommend that you also prepare an excellent general talk about microgreens. And if you want to be even more professional, you could hand the store owner a brochure outlining all the product's benefits.

Your job will initially be similar to that of a sales representative. You will probably have to canvass many grocery stores before you find the right ones. But you don't have to be afraid to talk to people. Always remember that all this work is necessary to start the business. Once you have enough customers, things will be much easier, and you might even think about hiring representatives to do the work for you.

Farmer's markets

The Farmer's Market is a relatively new format of conscious shopping, a good compromise between healthy eating attitudes and the need for fair consumption. Therefore, Farmer's Markets are a modern reinterpretation of the old fruit and vegetable markets, where producers brought their products to the square for direct sale.

In these contexts, small producers can sell local products directly and present themselves to consumers.

For a producer of microgreens, this type of market can be an additional opportunity. Still, there may be difficulties related to where you live, so you should assess your situation on a case-by-case basis. Therefore, if you are in a city where there is a farmer's market, I recommend visiting it to see if there are already other producers of microgreens and (possibly) take note of the prices they apply.

In some cases, going to a farmer's market can be risky because you need to carry a supply of a product you're not sure you can sell. So, you run the risk of wasting some of your produce. However, farmers markets provide you with an excellent communication opportunity. They allow you to introduce yourself to your audience and make yourself known in your area. So, my advice is to go to these markets, but with the same spirit with which you would attend a fair. It would help if you thought of it as a promotional initiative. During these events, you will find potential customers that you can approach for your direct marketing initiatives, which can bring you excellent profits, as we will see in the following section.

Direct sales

The last option available to you to sell your microgreens is direct sales. Warning: this is not a low-interest option. It may be the system that can bring you the most profits. Microgreens manufacturers who have developed this selling system usually require the customer to sign up for a small subscription for the weekly, bi-weekly or monthly delivery of a particular product. As you can imagine, this system has significant advantages for you, as you can produce only the quantities you are sure to sell (or rather, only those you have already sold).

MICROGREENS BUSINESS

As I said, to find your first subscribers, you can use the word of mouth that comes from your presence at farmers markets. But there are also many other local events you could attend and many different ways to promote yourself. For example, you could take advantage of Social Networks. Among other things, Facebook allows you to create ads that are only shown to people who live in your area and have specific interests. For example, you could target only people who live in your area and are interested in organic food, health, and conservation. Over time, you could build a mailing list or WhatsApp group to communicate all your future initiatives.

Direct selling is not as difficult as it may seem. Considering that you are targeting a mainly local market, it will not be complicated (and not too expensive) to take care of product distribution. As long as your business is limited (both quantitatively and geographically), it is better to avoid mailing (with the associated costs and risks). If your turnover is not very big, you can personally take care of the delivery of the products. It's enough if you have an ordinary company car and schedule one delivery round per week. Or you can choose even more original solutions.

MICROGREENS BUSINESS

For example, some manufacturers I know have bought a cargo e-bike to deliver microgreens to their regular customers in the city. The bike is also a great advertising tool because it's evident and consistent with the values that a company producing microgreens represents. I'm sure many people who see your bike will become curious and call the company.

The typical promotional formula involves delivering a mixed cassette of different types of live or cut microgreens. But, again, the more you pay attention to the details, the better your chances of success will be. For example, you could use only reusable containers or provide informational materials along with the plants to showcase your business and product.

If you use a well thought out mix of strategies, I am confident that you will find the correct number of regular customers and make excellent profits from your business..

BRANDING

Branding is one of the most intimidating things about starting a business. Branding is not just about making a product and giving it to someone you know or selling it. You need a brand around your product, and sometimes that's not so easy to do.

But what is branding? Quite simply, a product is what you sell, a brand is the perceived image of the product you sell, and branding is the strategy to create that image.

A unique brand can significantly impact your bottom line by giving you a competitive advantage over your competitors and helping you attract and retain customers at a much lower cost.

First, understand your target audience, mission statement, and the unique qualities that make up your business.

Once you can say with confidence that you've mastered these steps, it's time to move on to one of the more exciting parts of branding - visual design. We're talking here about your logo, color palette, typography (fonts), iconography, and other visual components.

Logo

First, you need a logo. A logo is a symbol made up of text and images that identifies a business. A good logo is the cornerstone of your brand. It helps customers understand what you do, who you are, and what you value. You will use or print your logo on all promotional materials, communications, labels, products, stationery and vehicles.

If you are good with graphics software like Photoshop, you can create your logo. First, however, I recommend that you contact a professional graphic designer. You can find many of them on a website called Fiverr, an online marketplace for freelance services with cheap providers from all over the world. Fiverr is very affordable because it has people from all over the world who have all kinds of skills, from graphic design to website design to marketing and advertising.

When you choose a designer on Fiverr, you probably want to jump right into their portfolio, but first, look at how they present and market themselves. Logo designers live and die by their portfolios, and their past work will likely be the essential factor in your decision. While some designers are generalists who work in various styles, many have a distinct voice and style or even focus on a single industry. And once you've decided on the perfect designer, you can contact them, and in no time, you'll have your logo.

Marketing Informational Materials

To sell your microgreens well and get your brand noticed, you need to create printed promotional materials. Flyers, business cards, brochures, catalogs, tablecloths with logos for farmers markets, t-shirts, hats, etc are all part of your branding strategy.

Getting your brand out there on every medium available is extremely important because it helps position you in the marketplace and makes you recognizable. Once again, this assignment may not be easy for you because you don't necessarily know how to create marketing informational materials. Not everyone knows how to design a brochure or knows how to create a flyer, and that's not surprising. Again, I recommend using Fiverr to find professionals who can do the work for you. The most important thing is that you know what message you want to convey to the public. Then all you have to do is explain your ideas to the graphic designers and oversee their work.

It would help if you also relied on a reputable print provider. There are likely printers in your home that are capable of doing the job. You can certainly look around and inquire about their services and prices. However, you can usually find better prices on the internet than in physical printing companies in your area. Just do a simple Google search to find many.

Vistaprint is the best online business card printer I've tested, thanks to its combination of excellent print quality, good design tools, and low prices. The company also prints promotional items such as mugs, posters, and even tablecloths.

Because Vistaprint offers such a wide variety of products, prices vary depending on the service. For example, Vistaprint offers glossy or matte business cards starting at 15 cents each ($15 for 100) and matte invitations starting at 72 cents each ($75 for 100). You can get a quote for your Vistaprint order by using the quote calculator on the company's website.

To get an accurate estimate, here's what you need to know:

- What product you want
- The size and style
- Any special features
- The quantity you need

You can test a possible design at Vistaprint by visiting the website and viewing the available templates.

MICROGREENS BUSINESS

PRICING

The pricing decision is one of the most important ones you will have to make.

As we have seen in previous chapters, you can get 8 to 12 ounces of microgreens (depending on the variety) from a single tray. Typically, you will not sell the whole trays, as it is best to do this business on a smaller scale.

The standard weight of a package of ready-to-sell microgreens is about 2 ounces (although much depends on the type of packaging), so you could pull 4 to 6 packages from a tray to sell.

The average price for a 2-ounce pack is about $3.

You can decide if you want to sell each pack at a higher or lower price. For example, some microgreens producers sell each 2-ounce box for $7, and others sell for $2.

MICROGREENS BUSINESS

The price of the product depends on many factors.

First and foremost, you need to consider the cost that you will incur. In the previous sections, I have already presented you with a general breakdown of the costs. As we have seen, the variable cost of producing a tray of microgreens is around $4. However, cases can vary, and only when your business is up and running will you be able to estimate your actual costs.

In addition, microgreens differ from each other. Seeds have different costs. The time to harvest can be longer or shorter. Packaging can be more or less expensive, depending on what you choose. All of these things have a significant impact on the final price you choose, so it's not possible to offer a one-size-fits-all solution.

But there is one more important thing to consider. You can't set a price by looking only at your costs. Of course, the cost is essential, but it's even more important to understand the acceptable price for the typical customer you're trying to sell your product to.

Once again, you can't ignore a careful analysis of your target market. Are there other vendors in the market? What prices are they charging? To whom are they selling their microgreens? To whom do you want to sell your products? These are all questions you need to ask yourself when setting your price.

MICROGREENS BUSINESS

If you sell your microgreens to people looking for a high-quality product with a well-crafted package and care about their health, you can get a higher price. However, suppose you only go to restaurants that use microgreens essentially as a raw material and don't pay too much attention to the packaging or other elements. In that case, you'll have to lower the price. Also, a restaurant may ask you to deliver an entire tray of microgreens every week. For these customers, you need to make a reduced price.

Your price choice depends on how you want to position yourself in the market, your costs, and how much your customers are willing to spend. Of course, the price can make or break your profit margin, but I can tell you with certainty that the business is almost always profitable..

MICROGREENS BUSINESS

PACKAGING

Packaging is one of the fundamental factors affecting the sale of any product, and microgreens are no exception to this rule. Truth be told, in the case of microgreens, the packaging is even more important than for many other consumer products. The target customers of these types of products are susceptible to environmental issues, so they will carefully evaluate the product you are selling and the way you have packaged it.

It is imperative that you know that everything you do in your business, including product packaging, impacts what can be called the "customer experience". Think of a customer who buys your product and takes it home but can't open it because the packaging isn't cleverly designed. Or think of a customer who opens the package, finds that it looks good, it smells good, but then finds that the box can't be closed again. Continuing with examples, think of your customer noticing that your product's packaging is made of non-recyclable and environmentally harmful materials. All of these factors can negatively impact the customer experience, create dissatisfaction, and hurt your business at the end of the story.

So what alternatives are available to you?

The bulk distribution uses a lot of paper and cardboard. These materials can also be recycled and are therefore suitable from an environmental sustainability point of view. The problem is that sometimes they are not strong enough to support the weight of a seedling containing moist soil..

MICROGREENS BUSINESS

On the other hand, there is also plastic packaging, but these are to be discarded in my opinion (although they are very cheap), as they are not very nice to look at and, above all, not environmentally friendly.

MICROGREENS BUSINESS

MICROGREENS BUSINESS

In any case, the choice of packaging depends a lot on the customer you want to target. Evaluate your market well before choosing your packaging. For example, a restaurant might accept a product packaged in plain plastic trays without any problem.

If you sell produce at farmers markets, you may opt for even more straightforward and homier packaging. In this case, your customers will love to see that your product is handmade, and you can package it that way. Many vendors who work at farmers markets bring the seedlings to the market, cut them in front of the customer, and put them in an envelope when they sell them.

However, if your product is destined for grocery stores and needs to be displayed on the shelves, you will certainly need to develop something more sophisticated. You also need to pay attention to design and labeling.

Transportation is also not to be underestimated. If the product is to be transported or shipped, you will need to opt for a sturdier packaging, and you may need to pack your already packaged product in a second container designed for shipping.

Bottom line: assess your market well first. Packaging has a significant impact on the perceived value of your brand, and making the wrong packaging choice can hurt your image. In conclusion, my advice is not to focus too much on saving on this element. An investment of a few cents in packaging can exponentially increase the perceived value of the product.

Labelling

Labels are an essential thing in your business: you can't have a product without labels. But most importantly, labels are a great marketing communication tool. There is much information you need to put on your labels.

If you have an organic certification that you've worked hard for, be sure to include it. Even if you are not certified organic, but you use organic seeds and soil, you can show that on your labels. Your microgreens are certainly pesticide and herbicide-free. Point this out, even if you are not certified organic, if you are 99%, your customers will want to know. Here's a sample list of information you could put on your labels:

- Brand Name and logo
- Product name
- Product image
- Certified Organic
- Pesticide & Herbicide Free
- Organic seed and soil
- Contact information
- Call to social media
- Weight
- Harvest date
- Place of business
- Washed or not
- Info on product use

Another thing to keep in mind is that each microgreen you sell is different and therefore needs another label. So, the best advice I can give you is to list all your products in an excel file.

I suggest that you create an excel file and put all the products that you have in your catalog in it. Next to the name of each product, you need to enter the information about the product: the photo, the weight, the instructions, etc.

MICROGREENS BUSINESS

Then you can provide this Excel file to the person who will create your labels, or you can upload them directly to websites like Avery, which I'll talk about in a moment.

You can create labels using Canva, which is a free online graphics editor. It doesn't have many features, but it's simple and easy to use.

Many microgreen growers create their labels using the Avery app (avery.com). The site is elementary to use: You can register, choose the size of your label, select a template (among the many available), and create your project. If you want, you can also import all the information from an Excel file. When you're done, you can download the label file to print at home, or you can have it printed directly.

How much you spend on labels depends on how many you order, whether you print full-colour or black and white, and what type of printing you use (DIY laserjet/inkjet, buy a specialized label printer, or hire a professional printer).

If you buy labels from Avery, the cost can be relatively high. For example, when producing a thousand labels, the price can vary from 20 to 40 cents.

MICROGREENS BUSINESS

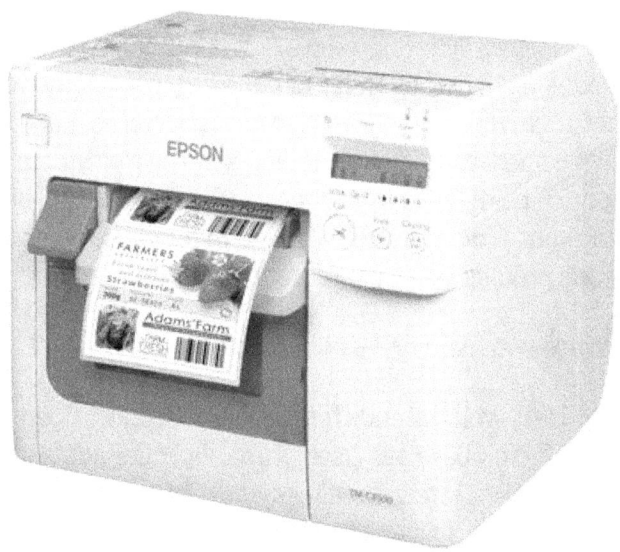

Avery is very expensive compared to a laserjet/inkjet printer, and I don't advise you to use it for an extended time.

A professional label printer can cost upwards of $ 1,500, but that's an expense you can recoup over time, as printing a single label cost much less with this type of product (about 4-6 cents, depending on the size).

Barcodes

Barcodes are another thing to consider, especially if you want to sell your microgreens in grocery stores. Barcodes allow businesses to distribute and sell their products in a variety of point-of-sale scenarios. Before you can begin selling your products, you will need to purchase a barcode for each product you wish to trade.

There are two main types of barcodes.

1. UPC, which stands for Universal Product Code, is a 12-digit bar code used primarily in Canada and the United States. Retailers add UPCs to every item they sell to track their product inventory.
2. EAN originally stood for "European Article Number", which is the bar code used by retailers outside North America.

The barcode issue seems complicated, but it's straightforward: barcodes can be purchased on the Internet, and there are many websites where you can buy them, such as speedybarcodes.com/ or buyabarcode.com.

Usually, you can buy both the UPC (for the US and Canada) and EAN (for the rest of the world) formats of your numbers for the same price. The price varies depending on the quantity. If you buy only 50 barcodes, they will cost you $0.7 each, but if you buy 1,000, they will probably cost you only $0.15 each.

MICROGREENS BUSINESS

Once you purchase the barcodes from one of these sites, you will receive digital barcode images for all of your barcode numbers in JPG, PDF, and EPS formats. You can use the images to create your labels or print them directly onto your product packaging.

MICROGREENS BUSINESS

MAKE YOUR DREAM HAPPEN!

You have now reached the end of this book, and I hope you enjoyed it and were not bored. So, I would like to say a few words in conclusion.

The microgreens business has some risks; as with any other business, success is not sure. But unlike many other businesses, it is possible to keep that risk at a low enough level. And that's true whether you want to grow microgreens to make a side income or whether you want to run it as your primary business. As we've seen, you can make a decent profit even with a minimal investment. And, more importantly, you can do the work in the comfort of your own home, using the space you may already have available. Indoor growing allows you to be protected from any kind of unexpected weather, so you can always be sure of a great harvest even if you live in icy areas.

MICROGREENS BUSINESS

As I have already explained to you, production is perhaps the easiest part of your job. It is the selling that is much more difficult. However, I don't mean to scare you with this. Some people naturally have a propensity for selling, and if you are one of those people, you will have no problem getting your microgreens to market. But even if you're not one of those people (or think you're not), I advise you not to get discouraged because you can learn marketing strategies just like anything else. Since you can run this business on a small scale, you don't have to recruit droves of salespeople to sell your products. Just set aside a few hours a week, and you can do it yourself. Or you could get help from your partner, your kids or some friends. Many people I know have started small family businesses, and I think it's a great way to share your passion with your loved ones.

As with all businesses, you have to do your best initially and learn hard to make things work. I realise this book doesn't have all the answers, but it's a great starting point. Over time, you will learn most of the information you need and understand for yourself what works and what doesn't. Remember also that every case is different, and what works for me may not work for you.

Whatever your idea is, I still advise you not to wait. The time to grow microgreens is now! The market is expanding, and the demand is getting bigger. Maybe there is no microgreens producer in the place where you live yet, and you could be the first. That would give you a significant

MICROGREENS BUSINESS

competitive advantage over those who come after you.

In the last section of the volume, you will find the information sheets of 20 different microgreens varieties that you could consider starting your business. Some types are easier to grow, others are more challenging or take longer to mature. I recommend: Do your market research before you start! Good Luck!

MICROGREENS BUSINESS

APPENDIX: MOST POPULAR MICROGREENS

MICROGREENS BUSINESS

1. Sunflower

Sunflower microgreens are probably the most popular on the market. They are usually easy to grow and only take 7-10 days to mature. However, they can sometimes have problems with germination, certain diseases, and husk shedding. For these reasons, they are not among the most recommended microgreens for beginners. Growing these microgreens in the soil is recommended, while growing them hydroponically is more difficult.

Sunflower microgreens are excellent in sandwiches, soups, salads, scrambled eggs and wraps. Both the leaves and the stems are edible. Try adding them to a sandwich to get the typical flavor of the seeds, but with the freshness and beauty of microgreens, or accompanied by cheese to add that extra touch that never hurts.

2. Pea

Pea microgreens are also very common and are one of my favourites. They are easy to grow in soil and take about 8-14 days to mature. They can also be grown hydroponically and produce a good yield.

Pea microgreens have a slightly sweet taste, with a bitter aftertaste. In the kitchen, they can add a pleasant touch of freshness to dishes to which they are added, giving a milder character and adding rich and natural flavours to any dish. They are great in salads or even quickly sauteed with some garlic, soy sauce and ginger. These peas are ideal for adding a touch of freshness and colour to salads, as well as soups and stews.

3. Broccoli

Broccoli grows very quickly and is one of the easiest microgreens to grow. If you have the optimal conditions, such as the right temperature, water and growing medium, these beautiful and tasty microgreens can be ready in as little as six days. It can be grown in soil or hydroponically and is perfect for beginners.

It is a robust and substantial microgreen that has a fresh, mild cabbage flavor. They are also popular for their health benefits as they are a great source of sulforaphane. It is an excellent choice as a base for any salad made with microgreens.

4. Basil

Basil is an excellent microgreen that can be grown for commercial purposes. All cooks know and use basil because it is an ingredient they use in pasta, salads and many sauces. Basil is the main ingredient in Genovese pesto. Therefore, you can sell it quickly because there is a good demand and cooks love to have an extra fresh product. It can be grown in soil, but hydroponics is preferable.

Basil seeds are mucilaginous, which means that when the seeds get wet, a gel-like substance called mucilage forms. As such, mucilaginous seeds require a little more care and observation than other microgreens. Because the seeds become sticky with the slime gel, they are often described as difficult to grow. They may not be the best choice for beginners.

5. Cress

Cress microgreens grow well in soil or hydroponically. There are several varieties, and it is a fairly well-known plant among microgreens enthusiasts. Its cultivation requires less water than most other microgreens.

Thanks to its distinctive flavor, watercress can be used in numerous recipes; add watercress to egg mayonnaise sandwiches, salads and soups, or use it to garnish canapés and grilled dishes. It can also be used as a base for sauces and condiments to pair with fish, especially salmon, shrimp and shellfish in general. They are often combined with ginger to obtain a mixture of, especially spicy flavors.

6. Radish

Radish microgreens are among the easiest microgreens to grow indoors and also among the fastest growing. They are suitable for any cultivation (in soil or hydroponic). Under certain conditions, they can be ready to harvest as soon as six days after planting.

Radish microgreens have mild sweet and spicy notes. They can make a colorful and tempting ingredient in your vegan or vegetarian sandwiches, but they're also perfect for adding to salads of all kinds. They are incredibly juicy, and for this reason they can become a natural condiment for various preparations (risotto, sandwiches, pasta). They can be added to salads to give them a stronger flavor, and they go perfectly with a crab salad along with cucumbers. Finally, many use them to give appetizers an extra touch.

7. Arugula

If you're just getting started growing microgreens, growing arugula microgreens is a great way to start. It's a popular plant with chefs and hobbyists alike, with a spicy, nutty flavor that will jazz up most dishes.

It also grows very quickly (both in soil and hydroponically) and can typically be harvested in about ten days.

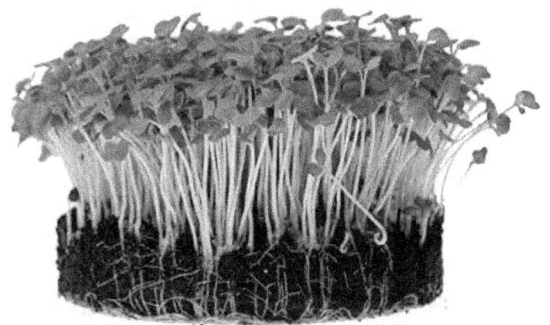

Arugula is one of the most popular microgreens because of its distinctive spicy, nutty, almost tart flavor that develops into a bitter and spicy taste. Arugula microgreens are delicious raw because when cooked, they lose their characteristic spiciness. Perfect for summer pizzas, omelettes, chips, pasta or rice. Its bitter taste makes it ideal to be combined with many other ingredients, including other microgreens such as arugula, peas, sunflowers and red chard.

8. Cilantro/Coriander

Coriander is a well-known plant, very good to eat and beautiful to look at. It is not one of the easiest or fastest microgreens to grow, as it can take up to 28 days before you can harvest. It is better to choose soil growing for this microgreen, as hydroponic growing can be very difficult.

Cilantro microgreens are suitable for raw preparations, especially as a garnish, as they wilt with prolonged exposure to heat. They have a bright, sweet and spicy flavor without the soapy, bitter character that mature cilantro can develop. Micro-cilantro leaves are most commonly used in Mexican, Indian, Thai, and Chinese cuisine and can be placed on eggs and egg rolls to add a bright flavor to lobster and crab, mixed with polenta, or even chopped into a sauce. Coriander microgreens go well with avocado, carrots, zucchini, tomatoes, coconut milk, citrus fruits, ginger, mint, lemongrass, chilies, yoghurt, chicken, white lamb fish and only need to be added at the final stage of a dish.

9. Amaranth

Amaranth is a microgreen with amazing color and flavor. It grows quite quickly, both in soil and hydroponically.

Growing it in soil, however, is a bit easier. It can be ready to harvest as soon as 12 days after sowing. It does not like cold weather, so it is best to grow it in a warm enough place. It can also suffer if exposed to too much direct light.

This microgreen has a robust flavor, similar to mustard, but much less pungent. Thanks to its tart but pleasant flavor, it can be eaten raw in fresh salads and pairs well with carrots, cucumbers, and radicchio. Its striking colors make it a great side dish or a delicious addition to any salad.

10. Beet

Growing beet microgreens requires special care and is therefore suitable for advanced growers. You can still put up with this extra work because these plants have many good qualities: Colour, mild beet flavour, and concentrated nutrient content. These microgreens are incredibly rich in vitamins K, A and C. They are also rich in protein, fibre, and antioxidants. Beet microgreens are easy to digest, so they are good for your health and in demand in the market. They can only be grown in soil and take at least twenty days to ripen.

Thanks to their blood-red colour, they are especially good for livening up delicious salads and adding sparkle to them. You can use them as a garnish to sandwiches or as an ingredient in numerous dishes, such as in savoury pie with beets and spinach. It is always recommended to use raw red chard microgreens to prevent their nutritional properties from being lost during cooking.

11. Borage

Borage is a moderate to easy microgreen to grow, but with a little patience you can get great results.

Borage microgreens add flavor profiles to salads, soups and sandwiches.

Young leaves with a unique flavor are an intriguing addition to a variety of dishes. In addition to great flavor and tender texture, they also contain many nutrients. Young borage leaves and stems have a pleasant taste and smell like fresh cucumbers with an aftertaste of cantaloupe. You can add them to sandwiches, salads, meat, fish and vegetables or use them to season sauces and decorate plates.

12. Cabbage (Cauliflower)

Cabbage is one of the most popular microgreens in the world. It has a pink stem, dark green leaves with purple edges and veins.

Cauliflower microgreens are easy to grow both in soil and hydroponically. It can be ready for harvest as early as 12 days after sowing

It is rich in vitamins and mineral salts, boosts the immune system and (as researchers found) significantly lowers triglyceride and cholesterol levels. They protect against cardiovascular diseases.

Its taste is delicate and sweet: it is excellent for enriching salads, sandwiches, pasta or risotto.

13. Kohlrabi

Kohlrabi it is often called German turnip. It belongs to the same family as cabbage, broccoli and cauliflower. It grows quite quickly, both in soil and hydroponically.

Kohlrabi microgreens can be grown in as little as 2 weeks. They are ready to eat as soon as the first leaves appear and have lavender stems with green leaves.

Kohlrabi microgreens taste similar to turnips, which may be where the name comes from. They are sweeter and a great addition to any dish. You would probably describe them as more of a sweet broccoli flavor. They offer a super high vitamin C content, so they have a slightly sour taste. Great for eating in salads, garnishing pizzas, or as a topping for various types of focaccia. Excellent, simply wilted in a pan, for garnishing canapes with liver and butter or canapes with seafood and raw garlic.

14. Turnip

Traditionally grown alongside carrots, beets and parsnips, turnips are one of the oldest and most popular root vegetables around and one of the easiest to grow in both soil and hydroponics.

The high levels of nutrients in turnip microgreens can help prevent many diseases by reducing the risk of coronary heart disease, stroke or high blood pressure.

Turnip microgreens have the right concentration of flavor, nutrients, and a pleasant and intense aroma. They have a taste like a spicy kale or spinach. They are pleasing to the eye and ideal to complete any dish.

15. Onion

Growing onion microgreens is easy, but somewhat slow with a maturity time of 15 to 21 days. It is recommended to grow these microgreens in soil.

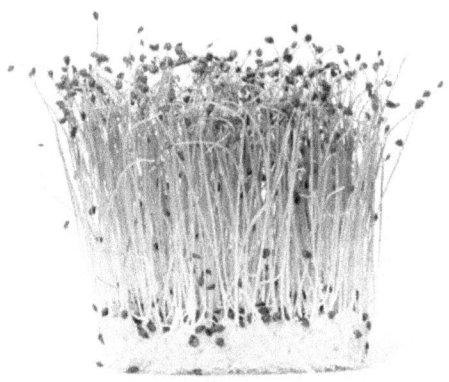

One great thing about onion microgreens is that you can get a second and third cutting from your first planting. Unlike most microgreens, the growth is from the bottom, not the top. The yield will be lower on the second cutting, but we think it's worth saving for another harvest.

Onion microgreens are a rich source of various micronutrients, especially vitamins and minerals. Some of the lipophilic vitamins are much higher in microgreens than in mature plants, and the vitamin E content of microgreens is forty times higher. In addition, microgreens are an excellent source of several bioactive compounds. Since onion microgreens are delicious, they can be used in salads, sandwiches and soups as an additional ingredient. It does not contain gluten and lactose and can be used by vegetarians and vegans.

16. Fennel

Fennel microgreen is easy to grow in soil and takes about 8-14 days to mature. It can regrow, so you can get a second and third cutting from your first planting

It is widely known for its licorice (anise) flavor, along with its sweet and peppery notes. It became famous in upscale restaurants in America in the 80s and 90s, adding a finishing touch to many dishes. Fennel micro greens are great as a garnish for savory or sweet dishes; they are thin, green and tender and have a slight anise flavor, making them a great garnish for Italian or Indian dishes. The special taste of micro fennel vegetables makes them ideal for summer salads or centrifuged.

17. Mustard - Spinach (Komatsuna)

This vegetable, which belongs to the Brassicaceae family, is cultivated in Asian countries. Especially in Japan for centuries. It has a mildly spicy flavor and is rich in nutrients.

Mustard Microgreens, like most brassicas, grow quickly and consistently under the right conditions. It grows quite quickly, both in soil and hydroponically. It can be ready for harvest as early as 12 days after sowing.

Its flavor is slightly bitter and peppery, adding a subtle note to dishes raw and cooked. Komatsuna microgreens can also be enjoyed by adding them to fried foods, pasta dishes and pizzas. Either way, using Komatsuna Microgreens in a salad mix with other vegetables, in a sandwich or lightly sautéed, are a very nutritious as well as tasty food source.

18. Mizuna

Mizuna is a green leafy vegetable native to East Asia, also called Japanese mustard. Part of the genus Brassica, mizuna is related to other cruciferous vegetables such as broccoli, cauliflower, kale, and Brussels sprouts.

It can be grown in soil or hydroponically and can be harvested as microgreens after 8 to 12 days or as baby greens after about 25 days.

It has dark green, serrated leaves with thin stems and a peppery, slightly bitter and sour taste like arugula. Although it is often grown for salad mixes, it can also be enjoyed cooked or pickled.

19. Nasturtium

Nasturtium is a trendy ornamental plant that also finds its uses in the kitchen. Its flowers, leaves and seeds are edible and valued for their medicinal properties.

Nasturtium microgreens are easy to grow in loamy soil with moderate water and plenty of light. They do not grow easily in hydroponic growing media. It is possible, though very difficult.

They have a peppery flavor and aroma and are delicious in many recipes including salads, sandwiches, eggs and meats. They are becoming a popular addition to sushi as they have a similar spiciness to wasabi.

The tasty and healthy young nasturtium leaves and sprouts contain vitamin C, beta-carotene and lutein. They show anti-inflammatory and antioxidant effects.

20. Tatsoi

Tatsoi Microgreens are another variety in the long list of brassicas. Like most brassicas, they are very easy and quick to grow, both in soil and hydroponically. Under the right conditions, they can be ready to harvest as soon as 12 days after sowing.

Their taste is similar to cabbage, but spicier. They have an aromatic and spicy flavor, but are more tender and sweet. They are perfect as a side dish to dishes of all kinds, such as grilled lunches or even your favorite dishes.

The tatsoi micro vegetables are also used to make fresh and very nutritious salads, perhaps along with other micro vegetables such as red mustard or mizuna. Sometimes they are used to enrich vegetable soups or to add an extra aromatic touch to sandwiches.

MICROGREENS BUSINESS

www.ingramcontent.com/pod-product-compliance
Lightning Source LLC
Chambersburg PA
CBHW070645220526
45466CB00001B/306